INCAN MYTHOLOGY

AND OTHER MYTHS OF THE ANDES

GREG ROZA

rosen publishing's
rosen
central®

New York

For Kathy

Published in 2008 by The Rosen Publishing Group, Inc.
29 East 21st Street, New York, NY 10010

First Edition

Library of Congress Cataloging-in-Publication Data

Roza, Greg.
Incan Mythology and Other Myths of the Andes / Greg Roza.—1st ed.
    p. cm.—(Mythology around the world)
Includes bibliographical references and index.
ISBN-13: 978-1-4042-0739-4
ISBN-10: 1-4042-0739-2
1. Inca mythology. 2. Inca cosmology. 3. Incas—Religion. 4. Legends—Andes Region.
I. Title. II. Series.
F3429.3.R3R69 2007
299.8'8323013—dc22

                                                                    2006000169

Manufactured in the United States of America

On the cover: Atahualpa (1502–1533), the last independent emperor of the Inca, was captured and eventually executed by Spanish invaders.

CONTENTS

INTRODUCTION

All members of a culture share the need to understand who they are and where they came from. While modern humans depend on science and religion for answers to their questions about existence, earlier peoples had to rely on their imagination and observation of nature. Myths are traditional stories presenting supernatural beings, ancestors, or heroes who serve as representations of certain ideas and character types. They are the response of primitive societies that sought to understand their place in the world.

Among the most colorful and enthralling of world mythologies is that of the Inca. The Incan civilization encompassed a wide range of customs and beliefs. The Inca called their empire Tahuantinsuyu, which means "the land of the four quarters." This name refers to the four regions of the empire that radiated out from Cuzco, in present-day Peru. Each region was governed by strong leaders who answered to the emperor. Tahuantinsuyu included hundreds of Andean tribes, cultures, and languages. The empire also incorporated the many myths of the various Andean peoples. These myths which evolved into a body of tales that we now refer to as Incan mythology. It is this process of assimilation and cultural layering that makes Incan mythology such a rich and complex brew of Andean folklore, history, and belief.

This map illustrates the expansion of the Incan Empire over the course of eighty-seven years.

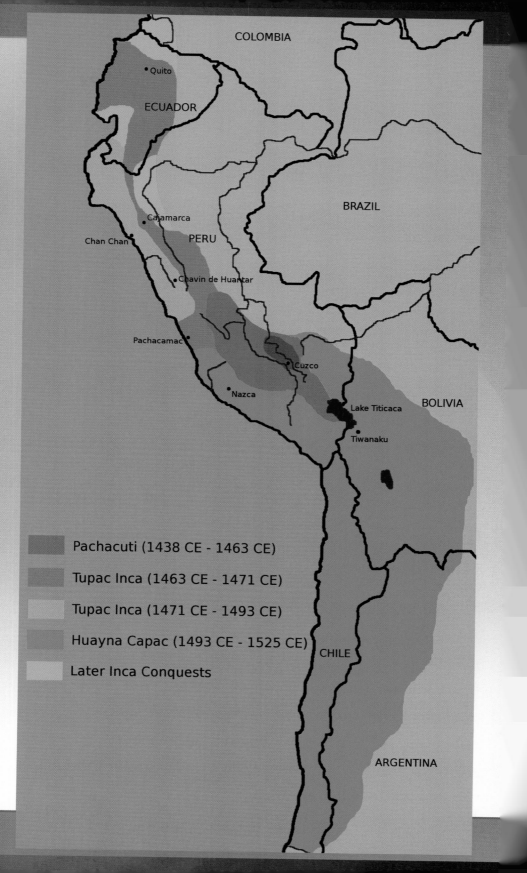

1 WHO WERE THE INCA?

Scientists believe nomads originally from Asia began populating the western coast of South America about 10,000 years ago. Living conditions in this area are harsh and rugged. South America's Pacific coast has been one of the driest locations on Earth for thousands of years. The towering peaks of the Andes Mountains line the entire length of western South America. This area also features ancient glaciers, active volcanoes, and fault lines that have resulted in destructive earthquakes.

Around 7500 BCE, the first settlements formed along rivers in the lowlands and on plateaus in the highlands. Remarkably, many cultures flourished here. Most of these settlements were small and isolated from other settlements, and the people that built them developed innovative methods of survival. The first cities began cropping up around 2600 BCE. These cities were usually uninhabited by full-time residents and were instead used as gathering centers for the purposes of government, commerce, and religious festivals. The various independent and isolated cities and settlements of the Andes region would sometimes be drawn into the orbit of one of the area's more dominant and powerful cultures. Empires of this kind united the vast territory of scattered peoples under a single governing structure and ruler. The first empire in the Andes rose and fell before 1000 CE.

Mt. Fitz Roy looms over a waterfall in Los Glaciers National Park in the Santa Cruz Province in Argentina. A large part of this park lies along the Andes Mountains. It is named for a huge ice cap in the Andes range. This is the largest ice cap in the world outside of Antarctica; it feeds forty-seven separate glaciers.

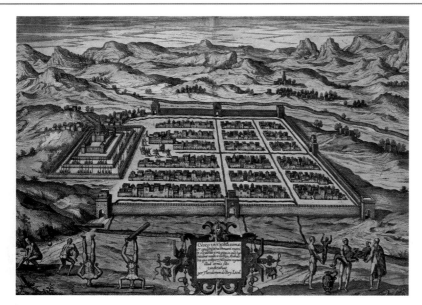

The Incan city of Cuzco appears in this 1596 color engraving. Cuzco was the center of the Incan civilization during the reign of King Huascar.

The Inca formed the most powerful and famous of the Andean empires. The first Inca settled in the Cuzco Valley of the Andes around 1200 CE, perhaps earlier. The first Incan village was situated at Cuzco, which would remain the center of the Incan civilization until its downfall in the early 1500s following the Spanish conquest. The Inca began as a small tribe. They survived for hundreds of years, mainly due to their location high in the mountains where few other civilizations could find and attack them. Eventually, however, the Inca began to thrive and grow.

Due to a lack of resources and farmland for their growing population, the Inca needed to spread beyond their central location at Cuzco. They were an aggressive, warlike people, according to archaeological and mythological evidence. So the Inca eventually began to control vast stretches of the west coast of South America. By the fifteenth century, they had formed a full-fledged empire.

Thirteen Kings

While much of early Incan history is clouded by myths and legends, most experts agree that there were thirteen distinct Incan leaders, or kings. (The kingdom centered at Cuzco didn't become an empire until the reign of Pachacuti, who lived from 1438–71.) The word "Inca" was actually their title for the king. It was the Spanish explorers who first used the name Inca to describe the entire people ruled by the king. The names of the first seven Incan rulers were derived from local legends of war chiefs and ruling dynasties. The remaining six rulers are historical figures. The thirteen Incan kings are:

1. Manco Capac
2. Sinchi Roca

An enthroned Atahualpa prepares to meet the Spanish conquistador Francisco Pizarro. Pizarro would capture Atahualpa in 1532 and use him to gain control over the Incan Empire.

3. Lloque Yupanqui

4. Maita Capac

5. Capac Yupanqui

6. Inca Roca

7. Yahuar Huacac

8. Inca Viracocha

9. Pachacuti (Inca Yupanqui)

10. Topa Inca Yupanqui

11. Huayna Capac

12. Huascar

13. Atahualpa

The Land of the Four Quarters

The Incan Empire lasted a very short time, from about 1438 until it was conquered by the Spanish in the early 1530s. During this period, the Inca quickly dominated much of the area that is today Peru, Bolivia, northern Argentina, Chile, and Ecuador, some 2,500 miles (4,023 kilometers) along the western coast of South America. Only the fierce tribes of the dense Amazon rainforest stopped them from expanding farther east. At its height, about ten million people lived in the Incan Empire, although as few as 40,000 of those people were actually Incan. The rest were members of tribes that had been conquered by the Inca. The Incan Empire was one of the largest and richest civilizations ever to rule in the Americas.

While the Incan Empire is sometimes described as totalitarian, the Inca usually allowed the cultural groups under their control to retain their customs and languages, including their religious beliefs and mythologies. After conquering a group of people, the Inca incorporated local leaders into their Incan political system. The Incan emperor treated the conquered people kindly as long as they pledged loyalty to him. This peaceful assimilation allowed the Incan Empire to grow larger than any other empire in the world at the time and to develop one of its richest and most complex bodies of myth.

Architects and Engineers

The Inca were a resourceful and clever people. The sophistication of their technology still amazes scientists today. Despite never discovering the wheel, the Inca created thousands of miles of paved roads, including hundreds of bridges and stone rest houses. One road stretched nearly the entire length of the empire along the Pacific coast. Mountain roads were surrounded by stone walls that prevented travelers from falling to their deaths.

The Inca were expert masons. Their buildings, especially those in Cuzco and at nearby ritual locations, were made with precisely shaped blocks of stone that fit together perfectly. Many Incan roads and buildings still exist and stand as monuments to the superior engineering and architecture of this civilization.

Farming in the deserts and mountains of the Andes region was often daunting. Using pre-Incan agricultural methods, however, the

Inca were able to grow more than enough food for the millions of people living within the empire. The people of the highlands built stone walls on the rocky slopes of the Andes and filled the spaces between them with soil. This created a series of steps or terraces upon which the Inca could plant crops and keep the soil from washing down the mountain slopes during rainstorms.

Understanding the Inca

The Inca had no system of writing. This poses a problem for modern-day historians who seek to discover what daily life was like for the Incan people. Written accounts of customs, religious practices, and warfare often offer the most insightful glimpses into a civilization and its people. What we know about the Inca

Terracing was an agricultural strategy developed by native peoples in the Middle and South American regions. Natural slopes, like this one in Machu Picchu, were modified to create small farm fields and allow for better irrigation. The result was that crops could be grown on otherwise inhospitable terrain. These crops included potatoes, which were a major form of sustenance for the Inca.

comes from several sources. Surviving written accounts of their culture come to us from non-Incan observers. Few of these sources can be trusted to be completely accurate, and thus the image of life in the Incan civilization is sometimes hazy.

When the Spanish "discovered" the Inca in the 1530s, many accounts of Incan life were recorded by Spanish explorers. The Europeans also preserved many stories and myths related orally by the Incan and Andean people living within the Incan Empire. In addition to these writings of Spanish chroniclers, artifacts that archaeologists have unearthed over the past 100 years reveal much about the Incan civilization. Figures and icons painted on pottery have helped historians piece together details of Incan customs and beliefs, including the content of their myths.

The myths, stories, and songs of the Inca have given historians an abundance of information about their origins as a people, as a powerful tribe, and later, as an empire. However, these sources are problematic for several reasons. Many of the Incan myths and stories existed in various forms among the tribes of the Andes long before the Inca rose to power. Over the years, as the Inca came to control the Pacific coast of South America and the tribes living there, several key changes took place. The Inca assimilated the tribes they conquered and absorbed much of their culture and beliefs. They often adopted the myths and legends of the tribes they conquered as their own. Furthermore, some older legends were altered by Incan emperors and other leaders in order to enhance their own position in the present and glorify their place in history.

Historians and archaeologists are making great strides in understanding the Incan culture. The myths and legends that have survived and been handed down to us highlight the things that were important to the people living within the Andes Mountains at the time of the Incan Empire. A fascinating and enlightening glimpse into the vanished world of the Inca can be gained by studying the stories that reflect and illustrate their beliefs and practices.

2 THE RELIGIOUS BELIEFS AND SACRED PLACES OF THE INCA

Religion provided a highly structured set of guidelines for everyday life in Incan society. The Inca revered plants, animals, geographic locations, and meteorological events for the influence they had on their daily lives. They used various means to keep their gods happy and to avoid hardship. Priests and sorcerers were a vital part of this religious process, as were festivals and rituals.

Religion was also an important political tool for the Inca. King Pachacuti and the Incan emperors who followed him convinced the people they conquered that the expansion of the Incan Empire was ordained by the sun god Inti. The supreme king, or Inca, was a direct descendant of that god. The Inca allowed conquered tribes to continue

An Inca sun plate appears above. Gold and other precious metals were associated in Inca culture with nobility, wealth, and political power.

worshipping their own gods and goddesses as long as they accepted that Inti was the supreme god and that the Incan emperor was Inti's chosen representative on earth and the Incan people his children.

The Inca often incorporated a conquered tribe's gods and legends into their own. Many tribes speaking many different languages were governed by the Incan Empire. These tribes each told their versions of ancient Andean myths, which were in turn absorbed by the Inca. As a result, Incan mythology is characterized by many variants of the same legends.

The Afterlife

The Inca believed in an afterlife. They believed that leading a good life would result in ascending to heaven—or Hanan Pachua—after death. There the Inca would enjoy an existence of comfort and ease living with the sun. Bad or evil people would spend their afterlife beneath the earth in Uca Pacha, a place where pain, hunger, and cold were unending. The Inca also believed that a person might prevent his or her soul from going to Uca Pacha by confessing wrongdoings to a priest and by doing penance. All nobles automatically went to heaven, regardless of how they acted in life. Commoners had to earn the right to go to heaven by obeying the king.

Sacred Places and Objects

The Inca worshipped their ancestors, the dead, the sun, their king, cultural heroes, and nature. They believed that many spirits roamed

Thousands of Incan mummies like this one were found outside Lima, Peru, in 2002. The 500-year-old Inca were buried in bundles of as many as seven people. Many mummies still had hair, eyes, and skin, and were buried with personal possessions.

the earth and inhabited a multitude of places and objects in the natural world. These sacred locations and objects formed the basis for much of their devotional practices. Some objects or locations were considered sacred simply because they stood out from others found in nature. The Inca called these sacred items and locations *huacas*.

Huacas could be holy places such as temples, tombs, bridges, hills, rivers, springs, and caves, as well as the monuments and markers built to honor these locations. Some huacas were charms or idols. Most households in the Incan civilization contained two or more huacas. The dead were often buried with them. Sometimes huacas were carried around the neck or in a pouch, especially by soldiers on their way to battle. This practice is mirrored in some Incan myths in which heroes are turned to stone and taken into battle to help defeat the enemy.

The dead bodies of some Inca—particularly important individuals such as kings—were mummified and kept as huacas. These mummies sometimes were seated at tables during feasts and were ceremonially served food and drink. The Inca believed that spirits looked after their living descendants, and the practice of "feeding" the dead was an act of honoring one's ancestors.

Ancestor Worship

The Inca believed that it was important to remember and honor their ancestors. All of them worshipped the kings of the past, who attained legendary status in the minds of the Inca. Historians believe that the first kings, Manco Capac and Sinchi Roca, may be legendary stand-ins for dynastic war chiefs. Incan kings and emperors who succeeded these two figures seem to have been actual people, although the stories about them were embellished to make them seem more heroic and successful than they actually were. Each of them are remembered and revered for their accomplishments. Some historians, however, suspect that the histories of the first seven kings could have been made up by the ninth king and first emperor, Pachacuti. They think he may have done this to prove to other Andean tribes that the Inca were the only true descendants of the sun god, and, consequently, that their culture was superior to all other cultures.

Ancestors were often heroic figures to members of Andean tribes. Just as most Andean tribes under Inca control continued to revere the gods they worshipped prior to the arrival of the Inca, they also continued to honor family founders. Family heroes were celebrated for settling the land on which the family lived and for establishing the code of laws by which the family lived.

The basic social unit of Incan society was the household. In turn, households were grouped together into larger clans or groups called allyus. Each allyu was made up of a numerous households of related families. Incan households and allyus kept idols made of wood or metal that represented their ancestors. Most even preserved the remains of their ancestors and presented them to the public during important festivals. Like the Andean peoples they conquered and absorbed, the Inca brought food and other offerings and decorations to the tombs of their ancestors.

Sacrifices

The Inca sacrificed animals prior to religious ceremonies out of respect for their gods. They believed that the priests could tell the future by inspecting the innards of llamas, guinea pigs, and lambs. Animal blood was often painted on huacas to honor the gods for whom the animals were sacrificed.

Although human sacrifices were common before the rise of the Incan Empire, the Inca relied on this practice only in times of great tragedy or upheaval. A child was usually chosen to be sacrificed in such circumstances. It was believed that the sacrificed child would ascend immediately to heaven and join Inti, the sun god. The child was given a drug beforehand, to put him or her to sleep. Most sacrificed children were killed with a blow to the head. In recent years, modern archaeologists have discovered the mummified

This Inca painting depicts a ceremony in which llamas were sacrificed to the sun god, Inti. This was done to ensure good crops and fertile fields, and it usually took place around the winter solstice.

remains of these children on high peaks in the Andes. The mummies, well preserved due to the low temperatures, have revealed much about Incan burial and ritual customs.

Cuzco: The Navel of the Universe

Cuzco was the earliest Incan village. It eventually became a city and center of religious and political power. It remained the heart of the Incan civilization up until the Spanish arrived. The Inca called

Cuzco the "Navel of the Universe" because it was the central point from which the four regions of the Incan territory extended. Many Incan myths mention Cuzco and other nearby areas—such as Lake Titicaca—as locations of great religious importance. Cuzco plays a key role in most Incan origin myths. The site on which Cuzco stands was said to be personally chosen by the sun god to be the homeland of the Inca, his children.

Machu Picchu

Ritual locations were important to the Inca. Cities were built largely for ceremonial rather than residential or commercial purposes. Many of them were erected high in the mountains so they would be closer to the gods. Perhaps the most notable of these ritual locations was the great city of Machu Picchu, which was just 75 miles (121 km) northwest of Cuzco.

Resting on top of a mountain ridge at 9,060 feet (2,761 meters) in elevation, Machu Picchu is a mysterious and beautiful place. Historians believe that the Inca used it as a secret ceremonial site. This small city features stunning masonry work, farm terraces, storehouses, temples, and about 150 houses. The buildings are extremely well preserved, given that they were abandoned more than 400 years ago.

Machu Picchu is home to several Incan observatories (places from which the night sky is studied). One is a pillar known as Intihuatana, which means "hitching post of the sun." At noon on March 21 and September 21, the sun is directly above this pillar and

Machu Picchu was a city located in the Andes Mountains, about 43 miles (69 km) northwest of Cuzco. It probably served as a royal estate and religious retreat. It has close to 200 buildings, which are now in various states of ruin, including private residences, temples, storehouses, and public buildings. The population probably was greater than 1,000 people at the city's height.

casts almost no shadow. These dates are called the spring and fall equinoxes and mark the two times of the year when the sun is directly above the equator. When the sun was directly above the pillar, the Inca believed that they were capturing its power for a brief moment. This astrological event was accompanied by a great festival in honor of the sun.

3 INCAN GODS, HEROES, AND LEADERS

Pre-Incan Andean cultures developed oral traditions that periodically changed depending on who was in power. These myths narrated the origin and history of their people. Descendants retold the stories, added to them, and transformed them into powerful legends. Great historic, cultural, and environmental events were recorded in the myths and legends as they were told over and over again, century after century. The myths provided the people of the Andes region with a collective memory that tied them all together and offered a shared history and religion.

The Incan civilization was just one of many in the Andes, and many had come before it. Incan myth and culture drew upon elements from these earlier civilizations. Over the years, the Inca rewrote the older tales to raise themselves to mythological status. As they began to conquer more and more tribes throughout the Andes, the Inca used myths to establish their connection to the sun god, helping to justify their rule over the various conquered peoples. They successfully positioned themselves as direct Descendants of the very same gods that many Andeans already believed in. In time, all people living within the empire came to believe that the reign of the Inca was ordained by the gods. In this manner, Incan rulers altered the collective memory of the Andean peoples and used it to their political advantage.

This early nineteenth-century panoramic wallpaper depicts a scene of Incan sun worship. Emperors were considered to be sons of Inti, the sun god, and were worshipped as gods themselves. Partly as a result of their devotion to the sun god and their seasonal festivals in his honor, the Inca developed a highly accurate calendar based upon the observed movements of the sun and stars.

The Incan Pantheon

Incan religion was pantheistic. This means that their gods were closely tied to nature. Just about everything in nature was related to a god or goddess. Since the Inca allowed conquered tribes to retain their customs, the list of gods and goddesses eventually grew quite long. In addition to the Incan deities, most non-Incan Andean tribes continued to honor their own traditional gods from the time before their conquest. For this reason, some natural phenomena are represented by multiple deities.

The Inca worshipped the sun god, Inti, above all other gods. He bestowed civilization upon the Inca through his son, the first Incan king, Manco Capac. The Inca referred to themselves as the "Children of the Sun" and set aside a large portion of their yearly crops for ceremonial customs involving the sun. Coastal Incas honored Mama Cocha, or "Mother Sea," for providing them with fish. Other gods represented the powers of nature, including the earth, thunder, and lightning.

Viracocha

The only Incan god not represented by a physical element in the natural world was the supreme god, Viracocha. Viracocha—sometimes called Pachacutec, depending on the region—was the god of beginnings and the one who created the world and everything in it, including Inti himself. Many Inca believed that he pulled the sun god, moon goddess, and the god of thunder from an island in the

Viracocha, a pre-Incan creator deity represented in this sculpture, was adopted by the Inca as a rain god. They believed he created the sun and moon by pulling the sun god and the moon goddess up from an island in Lake Titicaca.

middle of Lake Titicaca. Viracocha is sometimes represented by the waters of Lake Titicaca, or by a man holding lightning bolts.

The legend of Viracocha originated before the rise of the Inca. Many pre-Incan tribes held similar beliefs about the supreme creator, suggesting that a good number of the Andean tribes share a common origin. Some pre-Incan cultures believed that Viracocha was not the first supreme god. They believed that a god named Kon created men and women, but these humans were evil. As a result, Viracocha drove Kon away and turned all the wicked people into animals. He then created new humans, who showed great respect for their creator.

At different times during the Incan Empire, Viracocha was considered the supreme god, while at other times that honor was given to Inti. Some tribes believed that Viracocha was actually a descendant of the sun god, rather than that god's creator. These changes to the hierarchy of the gods were sometimes initiated by the kings and emperors and were meant to gain greater control over the religious figures—and by extension the common citizens—of the Incan Empire.

Incas consecrate a sacred vase to Inti, the sun god, represented by a massive sun disk affixed to the wall of the temple.

Mama Cocha

Mama Cocha was the goddess of the sea and the protector of sailors and fishermen. Some tribes considered her to be the goddess of all bodies of water, including lakes, rivers, springs, and even human-made channels. In general, Mama Cocha was more important to the people of the coastal regions because of their closeness to and dependence upon the sea. They honored her for providing them with food. In many myths, she appears as Viracocha's wife and sister and as the mother of the sun god, Inti.

Inti

By far the most important deity in Incan culture was Inti, the sun god. Inti was represented as a gold disk with a human face and sunbeams radiating outward from it. The Incan king was thought to be a direct descendant of the sun god. This helps explain why it was relatively easy for the kings to conquer such a vast territory populated with so many tribes in such a short period of time. They convinced other tribes that they had no choice but surrender to the will of the "son of the sun," since the kings' actions were ordained by Inti and expressed the will of that enormously powerful god.

The Inca honored Inti for nourishing all life on earth. Most festivals during the year were held in honor of this major god. Inti was the only deity to whom the Inca did not sacrifice animals (except during the Winter Solstice festival). They believed that sacrifices were pleasing to the gods, and in return for them the priests often received visions of the future. Yet the Inca believed that Inti already had everything that he could want, and therefore sacrifices to him were unnecessary. Since Inti was the god of agriculture, however, a large portion of the yearly crops were reserved for use in rituals and festivals involving the sun. There were only two major temples devoted to Inti. The more important of the two was located at the center of the Incan Empire, in Cuzco. This temple was known as the Temple of the Sun.

Illapa

Illapa was the god of thunder, lightning, and rainstorms (lightning had long been a symbol of power to the people of the Andes). Some tribes considered him to be the god of weather in general. Of all the gods, he was the one most associated with the starry heavens. Illapa was sacred to many tribes residing in the Andes, not just the Inca.

The Inca represented Illapa as a man with a club in one hand and a weapon called a sling in the other. A sling is a length of rope or hide that is capable of cradling a rock. A soldier or hunter quickly swings the sling in a circle above his head, and then whips the rock at a target, resulting in a sharp cracking noise. To the Inca, lightning was the whirring flash of Illapa's sling, and thunder was the crack that results when the rock makes contact with an object. Some Incan myths describe the Milky Way as an immense jug filled with water. Rainstorms were the result of Illapa hurling a stone at the Milky Way, which broke open and poured water down upon the world.

Mama Quilla

Mama Quilla was the moon goddess. She was the wife and sister of Inti, the sun god. She was also the mother of Incan founders Manco Capac and Mama Occlo. Many considered her the goddess of marriage and the protector of married women. She was also the goddess of festivals and the calendar. The Inca depicted her as a silver disk with a woman's face in it. The king's wife was said to be her representative on earth.

Some legends say that when Viracocha created Inti and Mama Quilla, he made them equally bright. Inti was so jealous that he threw ashes in Mama Quilla's face. This made her paler and dimmer than he was. Other legends say that an eclipse occurred when a giant jaguar in the heavens swallowed Mama Quilla.

Mama Pacha

Some people of the Andes revered the goddess Mama Pacha above all other deities. She was the goddess of the earth and of agriculture. Most Andean tribes believed that their earliest ancestors had first emerged from caves and were made by the same materials as the earth itself. As a result, many Andean peoples felt as if they were sons and daughters of the earth goddess. Tribes also honored her because she made it possible for them to sustain themselves through the planting and harvesting of crops.

Manco Capac

Manco Capac was the legendary founder of the Inca and their central location of Cuzco. The legends concerning Manco Capac refer to a divine hero sent by Inti to bring civilization to the Inca. The arrival of Manco Capac signified the end of a period of migration for the early Incan people, who had long been searching for enough

According to some Inca myths, Manco Capac is considered to be the son of the sun god, Inti. This is why he is seen here holding the sun in his hand. He was also the first king of Cuzco.

suitable farmland for their swelling population. Manco Capac's arrival also signifies the beginning of Incan history and the emergence of the first Incan heroes.

There are many different versions of the story of Manco Capac. The most common legends agree that Manco Capac and his three brothers and four sisters were sent to Cuzco by their father—Inti, the sun god—to rule and teach the people. Most legends say that Manco Capac ruled for forty years and established many of the traditions and laws that set the Inca apart from the Andean civilizations that came before them. Some historians believe that there was a real Incan leader—perhaps even the first Incan leader—on which the legend of Manco Capac was founded. Many other historians believe that Manco Capac was actually the name of a dynasty of leaders, rather than a single person.

Mama Occlo

Mama Occlo was the sister and wife of Manco Capac. She was also mother to the second Incan king, Sinchi Roca. Some myths say that Inti created her from the foam of the Pacific Ocean. Others say that she, Manco Capac, and their siblings emerged from Lake Titicaca or a cave high in the Andes.

In many versions of the origin myth, Mama Occlo is depicted as a wise and clever woman, while Manco Capac is honored more for his bravery. She is revered as the woman who taught the Inca how to spin thread, weave cloth, cook, raise children, and build homes.

Pachacuti

Recorded Incan history began with the eighth Incan king, Inca Viracocha. He attacked and drove out other Andean tribes to acquire more land and resources for his people. He also became the first Inca to conquer land outside of the Cuzco valley region. Viracocha soon began boasting that he was a descendant of the sun god and

Mama Occlo was considered to be a mother and fertility goddess. With Manco Capac, who was her brother and husband, she discovered and founded Cuzco. She also was believed to have taught Inca women how to spin thread. She and Manco Capac were chosen by Viracocha to teach and civilize the Inca.

Pachacuti, whose name means "world turner" or "world transformer," was the Incan king who transformed the kingdom of Cuzco into the Incan Empire by expanding far into South America.

that he had divine right to rule all tribes. This angered several larger neighboring tribes, who also claimed a divine relationship to their own gods. Two tribes, the Chanca and Colla, threatened to attack the Inca.

Some reports claim that Viracocha bravely defended his people from the Chanca. Most reports claim that Viracocha fled for the lowlands with his wives and oldest son when his army was pushed back to Cuzco. Another son of Viracocha's, Inca Yupanqui, stepped forward to lead the Inca in his father's place. Despite being outnumbered, the Incan army crushed their foes. Incan reports of the battle claim that Inca Yupanqui made rocks come to life to aid them against their enemy.

Inca Yupanqui became the ninth Incan king and took the name Pachacuti. He proved to be a brave and successful leader. He was also smart and ambitious. Shortly after defeating the Chanca for a third time, Pachacuti began to plan for the future of the Incan Empire. He continued an extremely successful mission of conquest. At the same time, he completely rebuilt Cuzco, creating a powerful political and religious center. When the city was completed, it was shaped like the revered puma and featured many architectural marvels that awed travelers.

The Legacy of Pachacuti

The successful war with the Chanca became legendary in the minds of the Inca. Pachacuti quickly became one of their most honored heroes. The ninth Incan king was perhaps the most successful military leader of all Native American peoples. He was also a brilliant political leader and civic planner.

In the years following the wars with the Chanca, the Incan realm expanded rapidly. Pachacuti established the pre-Incan language Quechua as the official language of the growing empire. By his order, the ancient roads were repaired and extended, and bridges were constructed to connect locations previously inaccessible to the Inca. Pachacuti initiated several other key developments, including improved systems of farming and irrigation and a sophisticated system of government. Many think that he ordered the building of Machu Picchu as a royal retreat or ritual location.

Pachacuti's son and grandson continued the expansion he had initiated. Topa Inca Yupanqui (the son) conquered present-day northern Chile, and Huayna Capac (the grandson) expanded the empire north into present-day Ecuador. Without Pachacuti, the Inca may have faded out of existence, much like many of the Andean tribes they conquered in the early years of the Incan expansion.

4 MYTHS AND LEGENDS OF THE INCA

Incan myths and legends obscured the history of the Andean cultures that came before them. Despite the great variety of the region's distinct customs and languages, many historians believe that the tribes of the Andes had a common origin. This idea is supported by the fact that the myths of different tribes have apparent similarities. Many myths seem to be variations of the same story. The stories evolved separately over the centuries as the tribes split apart, spread out over the Andes, and developed their own identities.

Andean mythology was passed down through the centuries by songs and stories performed in public during important celebrations and rituals. The myths and legends reveal information about the roots of the various tribes and the unique and pivotal events in the history of their people. The following versions are just a handful of what has been recorded since the Spanish first came into contact with the Inca in the 1530s.

Creation Myths

Despite the numerous versions of the creation myth circulating among the people of the Andes, nearly all of them share several essential characteristics. The similarities found in the creation myths point to a common origin for many of the tribes. In these creation myths, the people are said to come directly from the earth, whether it is out of a cave or spring, or from the clay of Lake Titicaca. This aspect of these myths may represent the effort by the ancient ancestors of the Andean people to develop agricultural abilities.

Lake Titicaca is most often the focal point of creation myths. Some of these myths say that Viracocha and his wife and sister, Mama Cocha, lived in the deep, dark waters of the holy lake. Others say that they lived in the heavens. Viracocha either used land from the bottom of Lake Titicaca or from an island in that lake to make human beings. Another common theme in is that Viracocha created and destroyed human beings because they were uncivilized as well as disrespectful to the gods.

One of the more common creation myths states that Viracocha and Mama Cocha lived in Lake Titicaca. Viracocha grew bored and wanted something to do. Mama Cocha suggested that he create human beings to keep him company. He thought that was a good idea. First he took clay from the bottom of the lake to make mountains and valleys for the people to live on. Then he used stones to create people. Because all was darkness at this time, Viracocha could not see what he was doing, and the humans turned out to be deformed and unintelligent. Viracocha destroyed these people, but Mama Cocha persuaded him to try again. So he created his own son—the sun god, Inti—to shed light upon the world. He also created his daughter, Mama Quilla, the moon goddess, to help keep track of time.

Isla del Sol, or "Island of the Sun," a Bolivian island in Lake Titicaca, takes its name from the Temple of the Sun, which once stood there and whose partial ruins can be seen in the lower right-hand corner. This is the site where Manco Capac and Mama Occlo, the founders of the Inca dynasty, were said to have been sent to Earth by the sun god, Inti. The temple was probably built by Topa Inca Yupanqui, who ruled from 1471 to 1493.

Then Viracocha created new human beings, again from stones. He placed stones in caves and lakes around the world. He breathed life into these stones, and they became the many tribes who roamed the peaks and valleys of the South American Andes. Viracocha left

his creations to themselves for many years before returning to see how they had developed. There are many stories about the humans and animals he encountered and the events that occurred. One of these stories says that Viracocha came to the Inca disguised as an old man. While other tribes had attempted to rob or kill him, the Inca treated him with respect and care. This made Viracocha happy, and he vowed to reward them by sending a great leader to guide them one day.

The Legend of the Twins

In some areas of the Andes, particularly the eastern slopes, the people told a different creation story. This myth may have roots in the ancient creation tales of the Maya (who lived in modern-day Mexico and the Yucatan Peninsula more than seven centuries before the rise of the Incan Empire).

In the beginning of time, a woman gave birth to twins, a boy and a girl. The father was a god. After delivering the children, the woman was eaten by a jaguar, which some versions of the myth say was actually her grandmother. The grandmother decided to raise the twins herself. She protected them from the "jaguar men," who came from a tribe of cruel and heartless people. When the jaguar men threatened to break down the grandmother's house and eat the twins, they escaped and fled to the heavens. One twin became the sun, and the other became the moon.

Origin Myths

Despite the numerous variations in Incan origin myths, they all assert that before the Inca rose to power, there was anarchy and chaos on earth. Men and women were uncivilized creatures who did not wear clothes, live in houses, raise crops, or honor the gods. The myths claim that it was the arrival of the Inca's ancestors that brought order and civilization to the primitive people living in the Andes.

All versions of the origin myth are based on this same idea: Inti, the sun god, wanted to teach the people of the earth to be civilized, so he sent a divine founder to lead them. In Incan tradition, Manco Capac was that divine founder. Some legends say that Manco Capac and his siblings came from an island in Lake Titicaca. Others say that they emerged from a cave.

The majority of Incan origin myths focus primarily on Manco Capac and his sister/wife, Mama Occlo. The myths say that the sun god looked upon the world and was disappointed and angry to see so much violence and sorrow among his creations. Inti summoned Manco Capac and his siblings and instructed them to walk the earth in search of the best place to begin a village. Inti gave Manco Capac

Manco Capac and his wife, Mama Occlo *(seated at left)*, receive praise from the Inca. The two have come to civilize the Inca and organize them into a community. The resulting kingdom that they created became known as Cuzco.

a golden wand and told him that he would know where to found his village when the wand sank into the soil.

Some versions of the myth say that Manco Capac received several golden wands, which he used to mark sacred locations along the route of his journey. It was not until one of those wands sunk into the ground that he knew he had found a homeland for his descendants. This location eventually became Cuzco. At this location, Manco Capac built a village and the Temple of the Sun to honor his father, Inti.

Manco Capac became the king of this new settlement. He gathered the men about him and taught them many things, such as how to shape metal into tools, plows, and weapons. He showed them how to prepare the land for farming and how to cultivate food. He also trained the men to hunt and defend their families. Mama Occlo taught the women how to cook, weave beautiful cloth for clothes, and raise their children.

All Incan kings were thought to be direct descendants of Manco Capac and the sun god. In their minds, this made the Inca more important than any other tribe in the world.

The Five Ages

The people of the Andes divided their history into five ages. Each of these ages is probably deeply rooted in ancient historical events. Yet while the legends and stories of the five ages became powerful myths in Andean society, the actual events that inspired them were forgotten and lost to the passing of time. The first four ages were

These illustrations depict the first four ages of the Inca. They appear in a manuscript written in 1614 by Felipe Guamán Poma de Ayala, a Peruvian nobleman of Incan descent. The text is a chronicle of the history of the Inca and an account of contemporary seventeenth-century life in Peru. It also serves as an exposé—addressed to Spain's King Philip III—of the injustices of Spanish colonial rule.

said to have ended in disaster, and the fifth age was that of the Inca. Many Incan constellations depict characters and events drawn from the myths of the five ages. Incan astrologers carefully studied the heavens for signs concerning the eventual fate of the fifth and present age.

The people of the first age were said to be very primitive. They lived in caves with wild animals. The first age ended in water (which explains the frequency of flood myths in the Incan religion). During the second age, people wore basic clothing, built simple houses, and established crude settlements. This age ended when the sky fell to earth. The third age was a period of growth and discovery. The people of the third age discovered how to weave, build houses, and plant food. They also developed their own marriage customs. The various Andean tribes began to communicate with each other, and it was a prosperous and harmonious time. Yet the third age came to an end, too. It was destroyed by fire. The fourth age was known as the Age of Warriors, or the Dark Age. Tribes fought with each other for land, resources, and power. This age ended with the rise of the Inca.

Flood Myths

Living in the Andes Mountains and in the desert lowlands was very hard. In addition to the extreme living conditions, natural disasters commonly made life even more difficult. Despite developing a relatively stable and effective system of irrigation, a cycle of floods and droughts created many hardships for the Inca. As a result, the fear of floods became a powerful element in the culture's psyche.

Flood myths are common to most ancient cultures. The story of the llama and the flood was a powerful myth throughout the cultures of the Andes. The flood marked the end of the first of the five ages and the beginning of the second age. Most Incan versions of the myth say that the gods brought the floods to destroy all human beings, who were thought to be incapable of being civilized. A small group of people—the ancestors of the Inca who were deemed to be morally superior to their fellow Andeans—were warned about the approaching flood. They moved to a place high in the mountains and were saved.

Another version of this myth relates that the world was once filled with evil, violent men who wanted only to hurt and conquer other people. In their quest for power, these men forgot to honor their gods. The people living high in the mountains were the only ones who were not corrupt. Among the mountain dwellers lived two brothers who were llama herders. These men were good people who honored and respected their gods. One day they discovered that their llamas were acting strange. The brothers asked one of the llamas what was wrong, and it told them that the gods were angry. The gods were sending a great flood to kill all living creatures.

The herders led their families and their animals to the highest mountain caves they could find. They watched in great fear as the rains poured down and the ocean swallowed the lands below them. The mountains stretched even higher as the waters rose, however,

Llamas have long been important to the Andean peoples. In the days of the Incan Empire, a certain kind of llama, the alpaca, was herded in mountain pastures and its wool was used for clothing. Other breeds of llama were killed for their meat, but they were mostly bred for use in the fields or as pack animals.

keeping the families safe from the flood. Just as their provisions were running low, Inti stopped the rains and the flood subsided. After the disaster, the people of the high mountains repopulated the world.

The flood myth demonstrates how the Inca understood natural disasters and why they occur. They believed that great floods were sent to punish people for neglecting to honor the gods in the proper way. This myth also explains why llama live only in the high mountains, since they remember the day when the gods sent the great flood to punish the creatures of the world. Other versions of the myth also explain changes that occurred to other animals during the flood when they were crowded onto the high mountain peaks. For example, the fox's tail was said to have dipped into the rising waters, which explains why the end of the tail is black.

Rock Myths

Most Incan creation myths describe their earliest ancestors as emerging from a cave or from the depths of the earth itself. As a result, the Inca believed they were made of the same rocks as those found in the earth. The resulting kinship they felt with the earth was demonstrated by the respect they paid to all rocks.

The Inca revered many kinds of rock huacas, from tiny stones to enormous mountains, some of which had formations that were said to resemble human features. Some rocks were thought to be inhabited by spirits or were once human beings who the gods had turned into stone as punishment for a lack of respect. There are also stories of rocks coming to life. Pachacuti himself was believed to have the ability to summon rock soldiers.

In many version of the origin myth, two of Manco Capac's brothers were turned to stone while searching for the sacred land that would support the Inca. This may have symbolized that the Inca had taken unshakable possession of the land, becoming organically rooted and fixed to it. It was also an indication that the land was now sacred. The brothers became a part of the earth that made up the Incan realm and were granted god-like status from that moment on.

Explaining the Natural World

The natural world—and everything in it—was sacred to the Inca. They told stories that explained how animals had come to look and behave in the ways that they did. Some myths explained environmental forces and meteorological occurrences. The following story demonstrates how the Inca explained events that occurred in the natural world.

In one version of the origin myth, the sun god chose a small, capable tribe to teach and lead the people. This tribe was made up of Manco Capac and his brothers and sisters. The leader of the tribe, Manco Capac's brother, Ayar Cachi, was a loud, strong, and bossy man. Sometimes Ayar Cachi beat his brothers and sisters or threw large rocks into the mountains that scared away all the animals.

Manco Capac's sister Mama Occlo came up with a plan to get rid of Ayar Cachi, and Manco Capac put the plan into action. He told Ayar Cachi that he found a beautiful llama in a deep cave and was unable to pull it out. Ayar Cachi boasted that he would bring the llama out. The arrogant brother walked into the cave in search of the llama. Quickly, Manco Capac and his brothers and sisters filled the mouth of the cave with rocks and then pushed mountain peaks over the cave, trapping Ayar Cachi inside.

The Inca believed that this cave was located about 20 miles (32 km) from Cuzco. From time to time, Ayar Cachi tries to escape his cave prison, smashing rocks and shaking the earth. This is why earthquakes occasionally rattle the mountainous homeland of the Inca.

5 CONCLUSION

Andean mythology has gone through many transformations over the centuries. The lack of a written language allowed the legends to evolve from generation to generation, and from tribe to tribe, across the region. Without written records, the surviving versions of ancient myths and legends are the best chance for modern scholars and researchers to understand the history of the Inca.

In lieu of written documents, the Inca relied upon a complex system of recordkeeping that used lengths of colored, knotted string called khipu. Historians think messengers carried khipu from outlying towns and cities in the Incan kingdom to the imperial center at Cuzco. The khipu may have been used to keep track of tax payments or commercial transactions. Historians have just started to understand the code used to create the khipu, but it is so complex that progress is slow. Still, many historians hope the khipu cords that have been preserved will reveal more than simple accounting information. They hope that they will some day shed light on the myths and legends of the Inca.

The Native Americans who live in the Peruvian Andes today are grouped under a single name. Although they call themselves Runa (which means "the people"), they are more commonly referred to as the Quechua. This is the name of the language they speak. It was Pachacuti who selected Quechua as the first

Though the Incan Empire no longer exists, native Peruvians—and other indigenous Andean peoples—still live in very traditional ways, reflected in their style of dress, agricultural practices, and commerce. Here local people gather in a village's marketplace to buy and sell produce and other goods.

national language of the Andes region. There are about eight million Native Americans who still speak Quechua in Peru.

Despite the attempts of the Spanish conquerors to eradicate them, Incan culture and language have survived and continue to influence modern society. The words "coca," "llama," "puma," and "condor" are just a few of the Quechuan words that have entered the English language. Quechua has become the most widely spoken of the Native American languages. This would never have happened unless Pachacuti seized control of the Inca and created an empire that rivaled any other in the world at that time.

The Quechua make up nearly half of the total population of Peru, and they have kept the customs and traditions of their ancestors alive. For example, huacas are still believed to hold spiritual significance. Many Quechua still farm mountain terraces and tend to llamas in the Andes, just like the Inca before them and the divine and heroic figures that people their mythology.

While the Quechua no longer practice the religion of the Inca, they have done an excellent job of preserving the precious myths and legends of their culture and providing a living example of a tradition that otherwise would be lost to time and conquest. In this effort, they have produced an achievement every bit as grand, rich, and enduring as those for which their Incan ancestors have been so celebrated.

GLOSSARY

anarchy A complete lack of leadership or system of rules.

artifact A human-made object left over from a previous era.

assimilate To absorb the culture and customs belonging to another group of people.

astrologer One who uses observations of the stars and planets to forecast human events and relations.

chronicler One who records historical events in the order in which they occur.

commerce The large-scale buying and selling of goods and services.

divine Relating to a supreme power or god.

dominate To rule or control completely.

embellish To make something more attractive or interesting by adding details.

hierarchy A ruling body organized by ranks.

indigenous Having originated in or occurring naturally in a particular region.

inhabit To live within.

inhospitable Providing little or no shelter and nourishment.

legacy Something transmitted by or received from an ancestor.

mason A skilled worker who builds structures of stone or brick.

meteorology The science that deals with weather and weather forecasting.

observatory A building or structure designed to help make observations of the sky.

ordain To establish a rule or order with religious and/or political authority.

penance An act that demonstrates remorse for a previous crime or sin and offers the hope of receiving forgiveness.

realm A kingdom.

totalitarian Of or relating to a political system characterized by strict control of all aspects of an individual's life.

variation A story or description that differs from other versions of the same story or description.

FOR MORE INFORMATION

National Geographic Society
1145 17th Street NW
Washington, DC 20036-4688
(800) NGS-LINE (647-5463)
Web site: http://www.nationalgeographic.com/index.html

National Museum of the American Indian
4th Street and Independence Avenue SW
Washington, DC 20024
(202) 633-1000
Web site: http://www.nmai.si.edu

Poqen Kanchay Foundation
Casilla 220
Cuzco, Peru
E-mail: info@poqenkanchay.com
Web site: http://www.poqenkanchay.com

University of Pennsylvania Museum of Archaeology and
    Anthropology
3260 South Street
Philadelphia, PA 19104
(215) 898-4000
Web site: http://www.museum.upenn.edu

Web Sites

Due to the changing nature of Internet links, Rosen Publishing has developed an online list of Web sites related to the subject of this book. This site is updated regularly. Please use this link to access the list:

http://www.rosenlinks.com/maw/inca

FOR FURTHER READING

Baquedano, Elizabeth. *Aztec, Inca, and Maya.* New York, NY: Dorling Kindersley, 2005.

Calvert, Patricia. *The Ancient Inca.* New York, NY: Scholastic, 2004.

Landau, Elaine. *Peru.* New York, NY: Children's Press, 2000.

Lourie, Peter. *Lost Treasure of the Inca.* Honesdale, PA: Boyds Mills Press, 2002.

Mann, Elizabeth. *Macchu Picchu: The Story of the Amazing Incas and Their City in the Clouds.* New York, NY: Mikaya Press, 2000.

Reinhard, Johan. *Discovering the Inca Ice Maiden.* Washington, DC: National Geographic Children's Books, 1998.

Steele, Philip. *Step into the...Inca World.* London, England: Lorenz Books, 2000.

Takacs, Stefanie. *The Inca.* New York, NY: Scholastic, Inc., 2003.

Wood, Tim. *The Incas.* New York, NY: Viking, 1996.

BIBLIOGRAPHY

Baudin, Louis. *Daily Life of the Incas*. Translated by Winifred Bradford. Mineola, NY: Dover Publications, Inc., 2003.

Brundage, Burr Cartwright. *Empire of the Inca*. Tulsa, OK: University of Oklahoma Press, 1983.

Corrick, James A. *Lost Civilizations: The Inca*. San Diego, CA: Lucent Books, 2001.

"Experts 'decipher' Inca strings." BBC News. August 12, 2005. Retrieved December 12, 2005 (http://news.bbc.co.uk/1/hi/world/americas/4143968.stm).

"The Flood Myth of the Inca." Metareligion. Retrieved December 12, 2005 (http://www.metareligion.com/World_Religions/Ancient_religions/South_america/flood_myth_of_the_incas.htm).

Gray, Martin. "Machu Picchu, Peru." *Places of Peace and Power*. Retrieved December 12, 2005 (http://www.sacredsites.com/americas/peru/machu_picchu.html).

"Inca." EMuseum at Minnesota State University at Mankato. Retrieved December 12, 2005 (http://www.mnsu.edu/emuseum/prehistory/latinamerica/south/cultures/inca.html).

Knight, Will. "Computer Analysis Provides Incan String Theory." NewScientist.com News Service. August 11, 2005. Retrieved December 12, 2005 (http://www.newscientist.com/article.ns?id=dn7835).

Markham, Clements R., ed. and trans. "Narratives of the Rites and Laws of the Yncas." Internet Sacred Text Archive. 1873.

Retrieved December 12, 2005 (http://www.sacred-texts.com/
nam/inca/rly/index.htm).

"Modern Andean Religious Expression in an Historical Context."
Portland State University, Department of History. Retrieved
December 12, 2005 (http://www.history.pdx.edu/hdwp/religion/
andes2.html).

Nishi, Dennis. *The Inca Empire*. San Diego, CA: Lucent
Books, 2000.

"Quechua Culture." EMuseum at Minnesota State University at
Mankato. Retrieved December 12, 2005 (http://www.mnsu.edu/
emuseum/cultural/southamerica/quechuan.html).

Roberts, Timothy R. *Gods of the Maya, Aztecs, and Incas*. New York,
NY: Metro Books, 1996.

Rostworowski de Diez Canseco, María. *History of the Inca Realm*.
Translated by Harry B. Iceland. Cambridge, England: Cambridge
University Press, 1999.

Sarmiento De Gamboa, Pedro. "Viracocha and the Coming of the
Incas." From *History of the Incas*, translated by Clements
Markham. Internet Sacred Text Archive. 1907. Retrieved
December 12, 2005 (http://www.sacred-texts.com/nam/inca/
inca01.htm).

Somervilli, Barbara A. *Empire of the Inca*. New York, NY: Facts on
File, 2004.

Spence, Lewis. "The Myths of Mexico and Peru." Internet Sacred
Text Archive. 1913. Retrieved December 12, 2005 (http://www.
sacred-texts.com/nam/mmp/index.htm).

INDEX

About the Author

Greg Roza is a writer and editor of educational materials for children. He has a master's degree in English from SUNY Fredonia. Roza lives in Hamburg, New York, with his wife, Abigail, and their three children, Autumn, Lincoln, and Daisy.

Photo Credits

Cover, p. 8 © Bildarchiv Preussischer Kulturbesitz/Art Resource, NY; p. 5 Wikimedia Commons; p. 7 © Peter Essick/Aurora/Getty Images; p. 9 The Art Archive/Mireille Vautier; pp. 12–13 © www.istockphoto.com/Feldore McHugh; p. 16 The Art Archive/Stephanie Colasanti; p. 18 © AAAC/Topham/The Image Works; p. 21 The Art Archive/Chavez Ballon Collection Lima/Mireille Vautier; p. 23 © www.istockphoto.com/Bryan Busovicki; p. 26 The Art Archive/Musée du Nouveau Monde La Rochelle/Dagli Orti; p. 28 Werner Forman/Art Resource, NY; p. 29 The Art Archive/Bibliotèque des Arts Décoratifs Paris/Dagli Orti (A); pp. 33, 35, 36 The Art Archive/Museo Pedro de Osma Lima/Mireille Vautier; pp. 40–41 © Alison Wright/The Image Works; p. 43 The Stapleton Collection, Private Collection/The Bridgeman Art Library; p. 45 Filipe Guaman Poma de Ayala, Nueva corónica y buen gobierno, The Royal Library, Copenhagen; p. 48 © Bill Bachmann/The Image Works; p. 53 © Steve Vidler/SuperStock.

Designer: Tom Forget; **Photo Researcher:** Amy Feinberg